Emerging Artist Magazine Volume II

CONTENTS:

Jonathan Boys, Editor in Chief
Autumn Anglin, Copy Editor

ISBN: 1468169149
ISBN-13: 978-1468169140

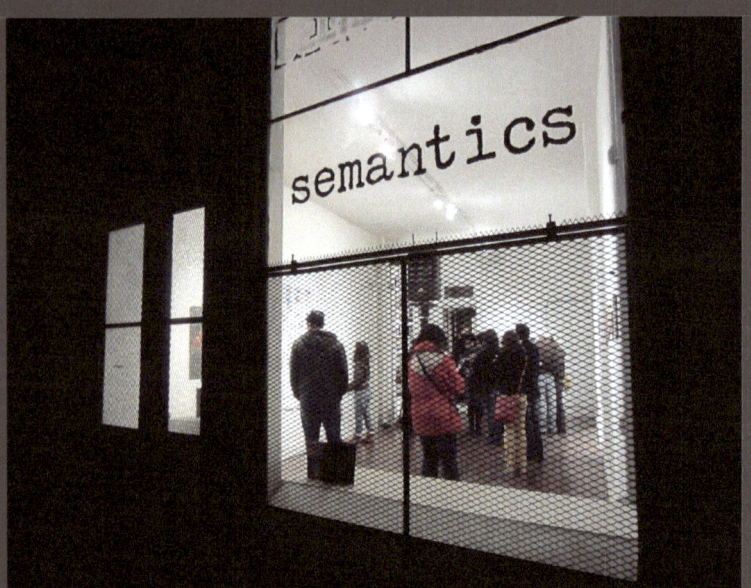

In Review: Semantics Gallery's "distance between _____." [approaches to contemporary drawing]

by Daniel Wolper

The Semantics Gallery in downtown Cincinnati had an opening for Art Academy of Cincinnati students on Saturday Dec 3rd, showcasing the work of 8 students. In its 19th year of operation, the Semantics Gallery is nestled in the shadow of one of the seven hills which surround Cincinnati, in the west end of the district of town known as Over The Rhine, so named because the neighborhood was bordered on the south by the Miami & Erie Canal, which reminded the primarily German immigrants of the time of their native Rhine River in Germany.

After the canal fell into disuse, the area was the converted into an unfinished subway project, and finally to its present configuration as a main thoroughfare. The Semantics Gallery is located right along this thoroughfare, nestled below the old canal right-of-way. Along this road, before the event, I pondered in my mind the history of this area. What must life have been like as an immigrant from Germany? What were the sounds and smells? There seemed to be ghosts whispering from the past from the buildings; the architecture still beautiful, but aged and distressed. What memories those buildings have.

Entering the gallery through the side of the building, I could whisper have those old ghosts from the brick grown stronger. Upon entry, the art of Lindsey Henderson greeted me. Her medium seemed to reinforce my feelings, and they served as a metaphor for the entire region. Her work consisted of old grocery bags, both plastic and paper, painted, with yarn strewn about coming from rips. It was as if the bags themselves represented the hopes and dreams of the Over-the-Rhine neighborhood, tattered and torn through neglect over the years, but still meaningful and beautiful.

After helping myself to a few grapes and cookies in the back, the next artist I moved onto was Megan Gertz, in the fore-gallery. Her work was visually stunning, and really one of the highlights of the gallery for me. At first seeming abstract, there seemed to be an order to the energy. Using paint and household cleaners to create chemical reaction, Gertz's work is reminiscent of the Hubble Telescope pictures of supernovas, and they also channel the energy of the churning waves featured in the work *The Great Wave off Kanagawa*.

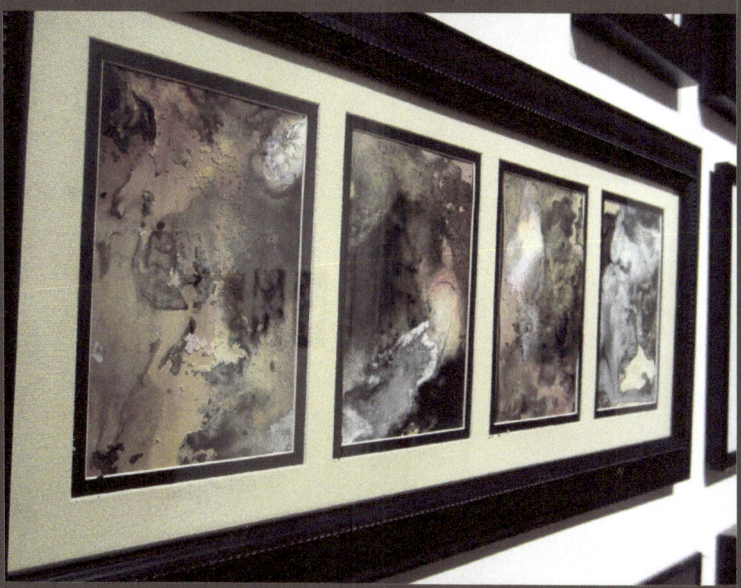

Photograph by Daniel Wolper

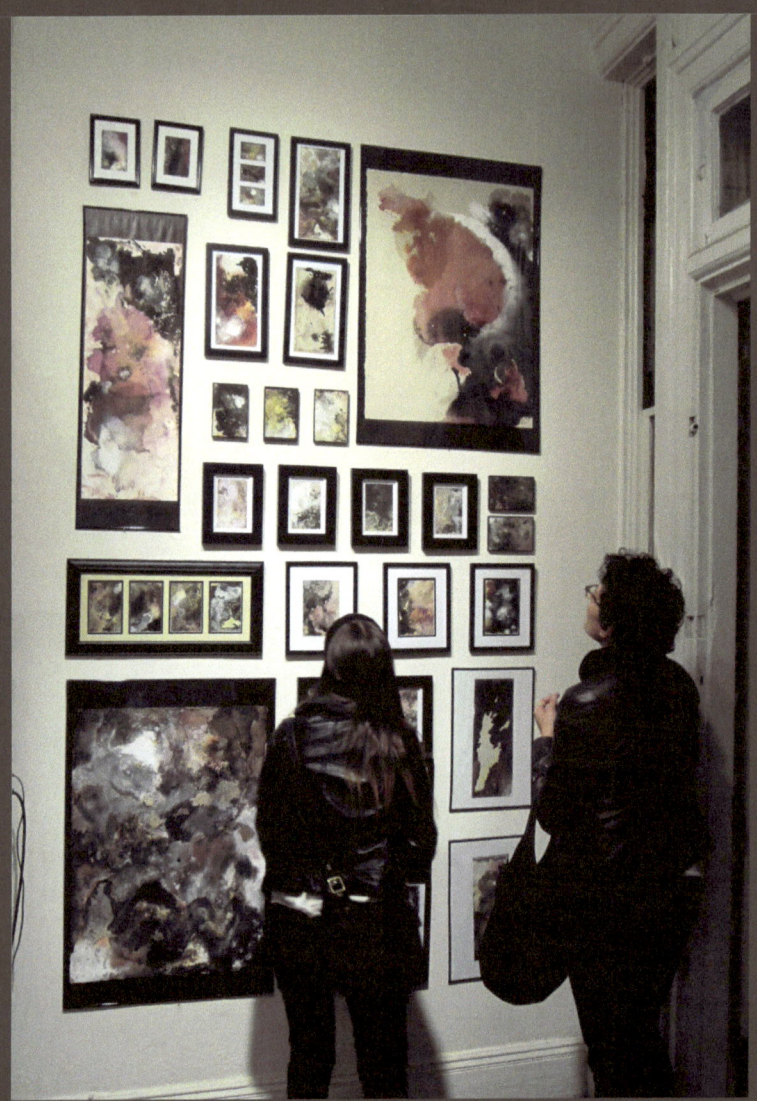

After that was the work of Evan Lautzenheiser. His work seemed to be sort of a work of educational anarchy. The viewer is bombarded with all sorts of information on a whole range of subjects. It is as if all the notes from any class the artist took were placed haphazardly on a large piece. The irony of the piece is that no matter how much one could focus on any small area, no sense of anything could ever be made of anything because of the sensory overload.

John Sloan's work featured a beautifully veneered piece of

wood, seemingly Ash, adorned with a collage of various images of people from around the world, primarily from the Middle East. His work seemed to perhaps reflect the spirit of the recent Arab Spring. A green line connects the eyes of all of the subjects of the collage, almost defacing them. They seem to lose their individuality and instead become anonymous in the context of the piece. It illustrates the power and personality that is communicated through one's eyes.

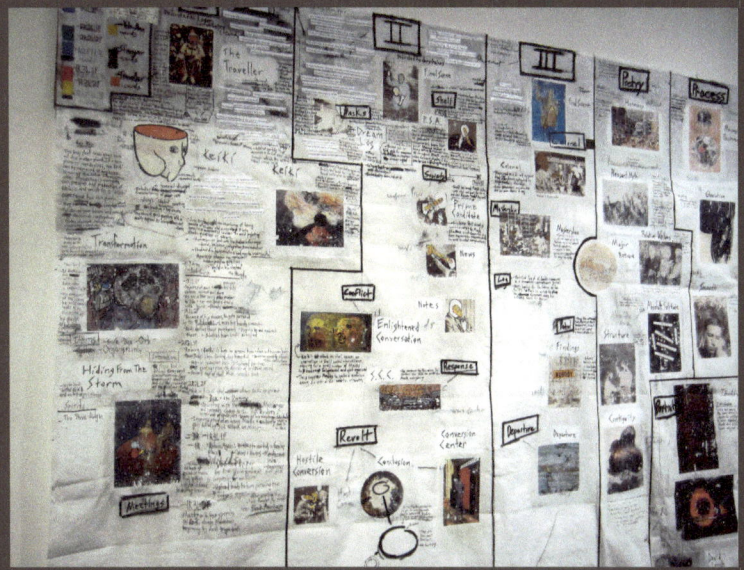

Evan Lautzenheiser

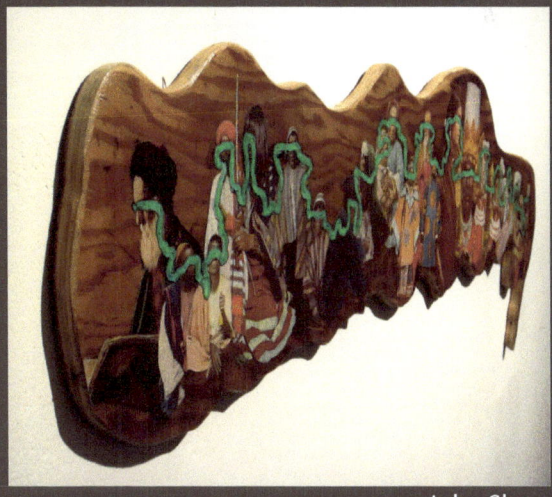

John Sloan

Next to that was the work of Hannah Graff, which channeled the dreamy world of surrealism, but in a more abstract way. Graff's work had both great color and contrast, and was both vivid in its detail, yet still non-specific in its subject matter. In many ways, it seemed to serve as somewhat of a Rorschach test for the viewer.

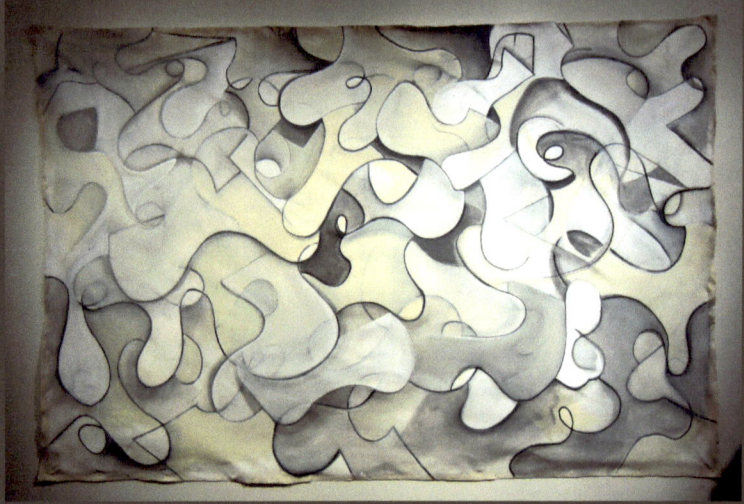

Next in line was the expansive work of Cody Gunningham. Gunningham made liberal use of the large space afforded him in the gallery. Calling his work a 'survey of the curves of time and space' he creates a swirling scene reminiscent of the work of Joan Miro. The churning scene created multiple layers of depth, even though the piece itself was in two dimensions.

Retreating again to the back gallery, there was the stunning work of Eunha Chung. Chung's work was another highlight of the night. Using Adobe Illustrator, she created patterns seeming at first to be random. However, as the viewer stares, things seem to become more orderly over time. This orderliness in the face of chaos seems reflects the artist's scientific inquiry which resulted in the piece. Chung states that she has recently been "visualizing some interesting related to the sun, such as... energy of the light and mass." One piece shows a series of rice grains to represent the mass of objects in the solar system, and their ratios. Her work proved to be both thought-provoking and visually appealing.

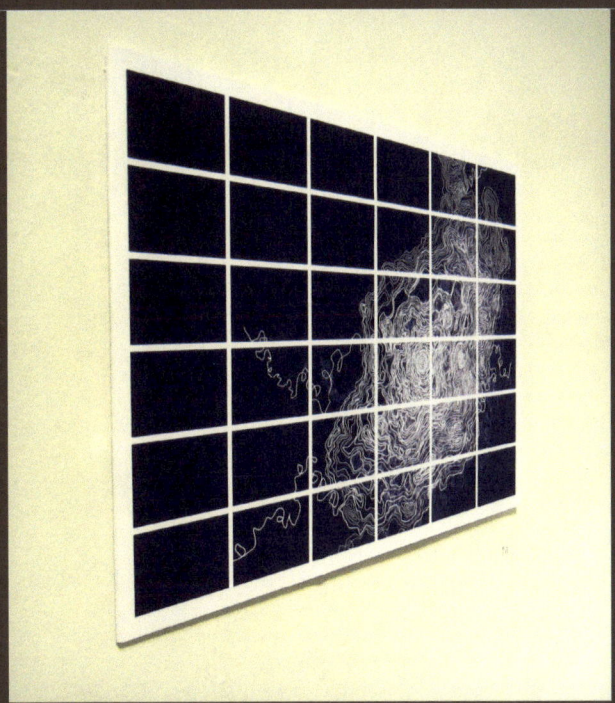

Finally, I encountered the work of Kerrie Houle. Houle's work was a series of printed paper with a story written on it. However, significant portion of each page has been whited out, leaving only fragments behind. These fragments serve to tell a story, one in which Houle describes as 'searching for a concrete, truth; something I can cling to because language has failed me.' However, as each page is pieced together, a greater story emerges. Houle's work reminds every artist of the difficulty of the aborted starts and stops that often accompany the creative process.

In short, the Semantics Gallery in the west-end of Over-the-Rhine is a great atmosphere to keep one's pulse on the heartbeat of the thriving local art scene in Cincinnati. The skills and talent possessed by those at the Art Academy of Cincinnati was quite evident, and it is great to see the future generations of artists and what they are expressing in a variety of different media.

For more information on Semantics Gallery go to: **www.facebook.com/semanticsgallery**

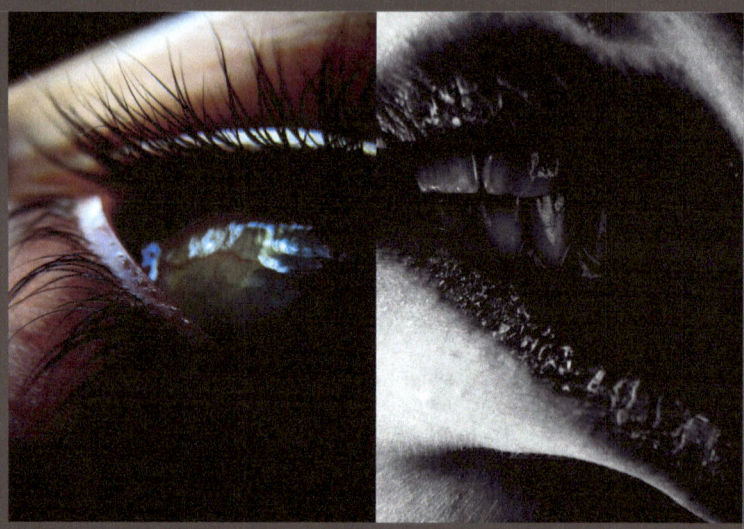

And the River Will Rise Up
by Samantha Hulbert, a.k.a. God Volcano

It was in 2006 when I picked up my first camera, a Pentax ZX-50, which was given to me by my father. The camera was a second limb. And I took it everywhere with me, which in turn created a drive that would never truly subside. For about a year, I had a pile of prints depicting everything from portraits of my closest friends to the macros of the flowers outside in my backyard. It was until I got my first digital camera, a Canon Powershot S3IS, that I really started thriving, really wanting to learn how to better create an image. Yes, these were just the beginning stages of a long, fulfilling relationship with photography.

I was born in Ashtabula, Ohio and moved all around from there on out. My childhood was based in Florida; but from the ages of seven to twenty-one, I lived in North Carolina. Those last four years of living there, I could feel the drive that was all too prevalent from the years before had dwindled. Everything was a routine, and I became complacent, making no time for artistic expression. I was not growing anymore. I was stagnating, repressing the drive to create. In retrospect, I should've made the move far sooner, but I finally got out of the cesspool I was living in and made the long move from North Carolina to the beautiful West Coast.

Portland, Oregon was the air I needed to breathe in order to get back to where my mindset was so long ago. All of the new surroundings, the eclectic groups of people, the overall air of creativity that thrives here kick started a new era for me.

When I first started taking photographs, I now know I held back from what I was truly capable of showcasing. Perhaps it was out of fear of not truly being accepted, or perhaps it was something as simple as immaturity and lack of skill. I was in a shell. And slowly, day by day, I'd chip away the pieces, eventually breaking out of the constraints I'd given myself. The use of bold colors and shadows, self portraiture, and a fascination with nature have always been on-going components through out my portfolio. But with the progression of time brings change - with new experiences brings growth; styles are subsequently redefined. From naivety to bold defiance, my photography became not so much about *taking* photos, but creating (by any means necessary) a true representation of myself, what I love, and what I've been through.

As far as everything I've learned about techniques and aesthetic appeal, I've learned the majority of it on my own. And as hard as it is to admit, I would still have to consider myself an amateur because of that and the fact that I've never had any real formal schooling. Personally and artistically, however, I'm always in the pursuit of knowledge. I'm constantly learning new things even after six years of photography. And I owe it partly to never sticking to one concept or the same subject matter. In doing so, it creates a lovely rift in an otherwise bland routine.

From the *very* beginning, I've used music as an inspiration. The first real self portrait I ever took (that I was genuinely proud of) was in 2007 entitled *Go Back to Sleep* (from A Perfect Circle's The Thirteenth Step): a black and white piece with heavy shadows and bright highlights to outline skin and bone. I'm cradled in my favorite chair with my head buried down and my left hand resting at the very top. Regardless of how long ago it was taken or the amateurish editing, I still consider it to be perfect. It was a catalyst, a culmination of everything that I am, and, most importantly, a glimpse of what was to become of my photography.

God Volcano or Volcano is a pseudonym of mine that I coined after falling in love with the work of Pig (aka Raymond Watts). Not only does the name tie into my love of music and the song itself, but it has a bit of a deeper, more personal meaning - when speaking metaphorically, of course, I'm a volcano. I have emotions, some bottled up, some latent. It's incredibly difficult to repress emotions for me; but when I do, it's only a matter of time before I burst. And then there's destruction and ending of relationships, bridges are burned, anger is at its peak. On the other hand, when I'm able to talk things out or speak freely without any fear of judgment or confrontation - I'm dormant. I'm solidified. I'm serene, beautiful, just as a volcano would be. As far as "God" Volcano, I liken it to audible confidence. For the majority of my schooling, I was the center for ridicule, so I never had any room to have self-confidence. I've always been that kind of person to retreat inward. But I've come such a long way in terms of, well, everything - photography, acquiring knowledge, learning to better myself as a human being. Photography itself gave me the confidence I've been looking for, made me realize things about myself and even others. It's true - we are not all perfect. But the only thing we *can* do is accept, never dwell, and grow with it, always with confidence.

TTIDFL II: *The Things I Do For Love*, is a more recent portrait taken in October 2011. There's a photo *TTIDFL I* that goes along with this, as well, which is a macro of my mouth housing copious amounts of dry dirt and debris.

While a photograph of a beautiful landscape is indeed beautiful, it still holds no substance. So I created this piece, something that can hopefully warrant an emotional response, something to make a person ask themselves, "Well, why? Why would you do that?" like creating something new, something no one else would think/want to do for a photograph. I take pride in the process, the pain, the time, and (in this case) the dry heaving it takes to have something turn out the way I envision it.

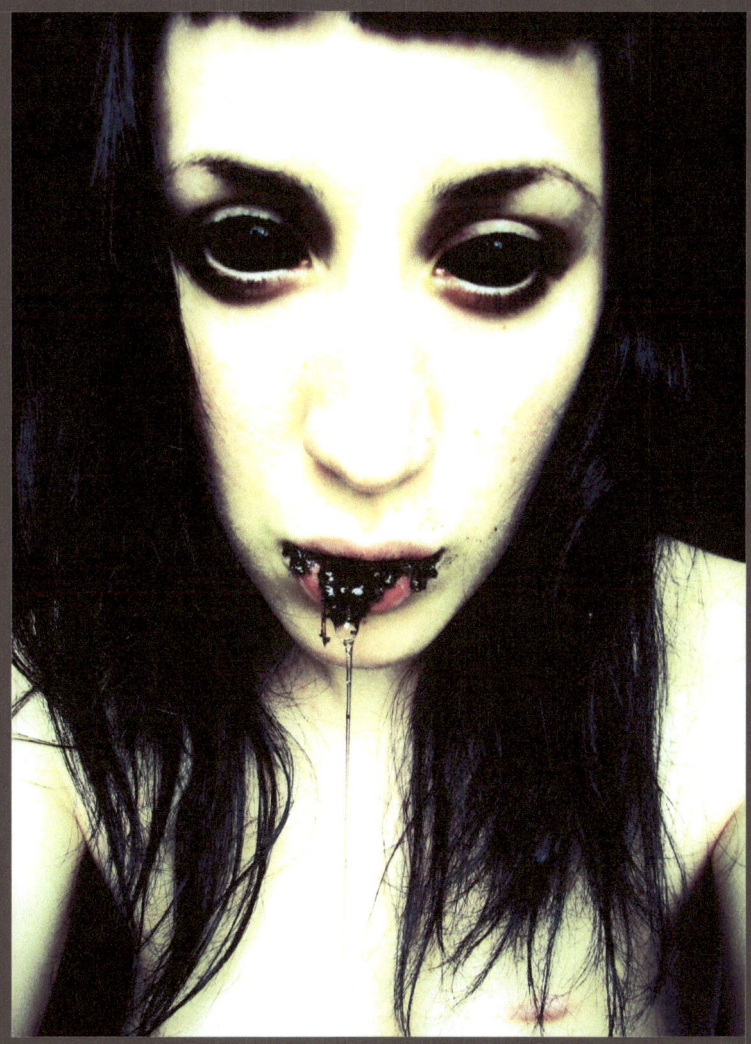

And all of that ties into the whole title: with love comes sacrifice. I sacrifice possible ridicule and judgment for the image, but I do it for the love of art and creation.

With some portraits, I do use a flash. But for the majority of the time (and in this case), I used natural light. With regards to editing - I used two filters, some mild retouching of the skin, and heavy use of the burn tool.

The black sclera look is a new addition to my self portraits. I've altered my eyes this way because, in reality, I have incredibly weak eye muscles, which causes one to drift.

In much older portraits, you would never find my face directed towards the camera; only a profile was visible or my hair would perfectly sweep across my face for concealment. With the black sclera, I open myself up to more ways to express an emotion; gaze can finally be achieved even with the lack of an iris.

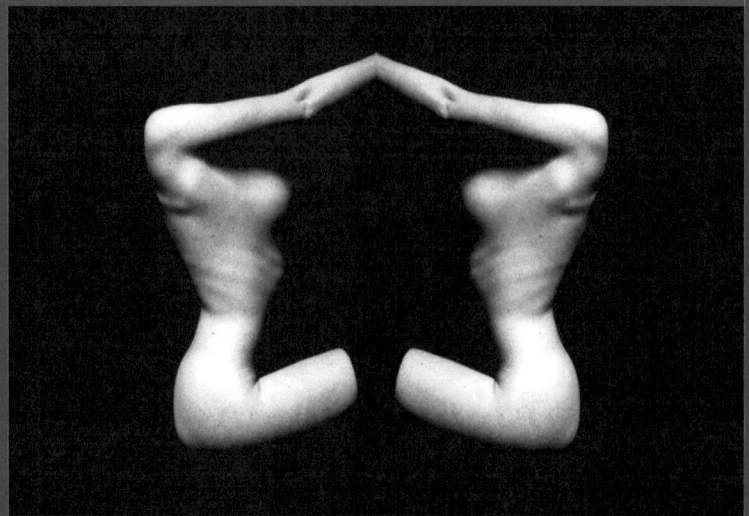

SYMBOLS: My creative process varies. For instance, with *TTIDFL*, I knew what I wanted the final product to look like. So it's as simple as taking about two dozen photographs, then finishing off with proper editing. *Symbols*, however, I went in without anything specific in mind. I was just posing my body the way I saw fit, hoping I'd get the right shot. And then came the editing - once I started to black out the entire image, I realized it wasn't strong enough on its own. So I was able to (visually) piece the photo with its mirror image in order to create something with far more depth. It's as if my subconscious mind did the creating.

I've always been fascinated by double imagery, especially when coupled like this as it creates an entirely new image. The fact that this is reminiscent of an inkblot ties back loosely to the whole subconscious aspect. Of course, there was *some* thought behind the whole process because I know what poses and angles work for my body type; there was attention to lighting, etc. But, for the most part, I went in blindly. Yet, personal symbolism still seemed to manifest itself, creating a concept I never knew could exist.

Symbols was just the catalyst for a new means of expression. Not all photographs can work perfectly in creating latent symbolism, but I started to become much more aware of the unique shapes that had the potential of creating such an image. Pieces such as *Burn, When the Clouds Appeared, Lineage*, and many other pieces were also created with this unique mindset.

Attention to every single detail, every angle, every flaw is pertinent to ensuring a worthwhile final product. I have the ability to erase and cover up superfluous, unwanted components, sure. But ultimately, the photograph will always be in it's original form, the way it was meant to be. Each and every piece has a concept, a deeper meaning, whether it's intentional or not.

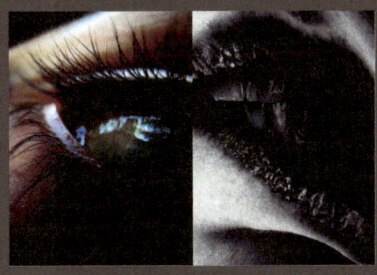

WRECKED: I love Nature, Landscape, and Portrait photography, although I love capturing most of everything. Macro, however, is by far my favorite. I can't help but finding pleasure in capturing the intricacies that people aren't usually able to see. For example, the human eye - they're expressive, a way to speak volumes without the mention of a single word. The iris alone is architectural, uniquely structured for the person housing them. The human body's "window to the soul", so beautiful crafted with its combinations of deep crevices and cracks, spots, and waves. Simply put, the human eye is a piece of artwork. And I look to capture it. I've always had an oral and ocular fixation, though I can't truly explain why. I will say, however, that with childhood comes memories. And my memories of childhood comes with trauma: when I was about four years old, I had surgery on my eyes. Doctors had to literally pop them out of their sockets in order to twist the muscles together in hopes of strengthening them. Long story short, my eyes never strengthened, and I've been plagued with weak eye muscles for twenty years. Just as mentioned in the beginning, I've carried this stigma around with me. It's been difficult in overcoming something I can't change.

At an early age, I was self-conscious about my mouth, as well. I had a large gap in between my two front teeth that I thought I'd never outgrow. By the age of ten, give or take a few years, it started to close up. And it didn't take long after that for the gap to be non-existent.

Wrecked was taken around early 2011, when my personal style truly started to form. It's as if everything from the years before never mattered. I'd finally grown out of that shell and (to put it bluntly) said, "I don't give a fuck anymore. This is who I am." I started to embrace the shape of my body and everything I once thought was a flaw turned into significance. *Wrecked* is all about confronting my fears and memories head on through the use of a camera lens. I made myself vulnerable, to an extent, but I wasn't afraid to showcase it - the eyes became a voice; the mouth became a symbol of power and strength.

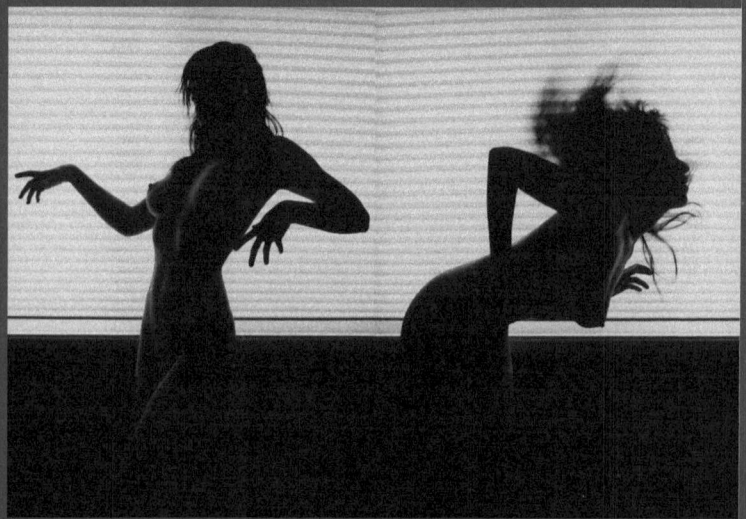

DON'T LET IT GO: August, 2011 - At this point in time, I was in a creative rut: my camera was temporarily out of commission; my mind was scattered, unable to come up with any real concept or image that was truly genuine. It happens sometimes. I get to this point where I can't produce any more. And if I try to create in this stage, I'm dissatisfied with anything and everything. Photos will then start to look the same, and that's something I try so desperately to avoid, especially with my self-portraiture.

I've learned to wait, to give myself some time to really come up with something unique and, most importantly, something that actually *means* something to me. However, I can only go so long before I start to feel this pressure build up in my chest. Emotions and thoughts start to build and build, and when I'm at the peak of it all - that's when I know I'm ready to create.

Music will always be incorporated in someway, somehow to most (if not all) of my self-portraits.

For this piece I knew I wanted color, as many of the portraits before this were mainly black and white. The blue tones, which are colors most prevalent within my body of work, were chosen for a few reasons: the song *Blue* from A Perfect Circle is forever circling in my mind. Along with that, the blue seamlessly goes hand in hand with the melancholic facial expressions.

A prominent component within my self portraits is movement. It not only adds more depth and substance, but visually, I find it more stimulating than just the static form of a body. I will say, however, that on a more cognitive level - movement is the only constant in life. I find myself dwelling on the fact that nothing lasts. People, relationships, the trees outside, even the largest rocks on Earth can't stand the test of time. But by capturing this very moment of movement, I was able to create something that's forever constant, never to change.

For six years now, I've been taking photographs - documenting as much of my life as possible. Capturing the highs, the lows, and the deep unforgiving lows. What better purpose would a camera have if you couldn't create something tangible to keep with you until the day you die? To remember your youth and where you lived three years ago? To capture a moment you know you'd never see again?

Just in this past year alone, I've been through so much. I'm fortunate for the place I'm at right now, but it took me so long to get here. Really, though, whatever happens in life, it shapes you - living in a shit hole apartment with shit people; getting ridiculed for what you look like; moving to a completely new, foreign city; heartbreak, lies, and love. I've been through enough to know that anything can be overcome as long you have confidence, family, and *good* people in your life. And it always helps to have something you love doing, something that brings happiness to an otherwise dull life.

I was born to have a camera in my hand; I have too much to say and feel and think to really have it any other way. Whatever I have to do to keep learning, to keep pushing myself to work harder and out do myself - I'll do it because I strive for something more. I want to go places, travel, meet new people, go on tour with a band to be their personal photographer, get my own studio, just experience *new* things. Twenty three years I've been on this Earth, and I've already learned so much, so I know I've got some time. And with time comes knowledge. And with knowledge comes success. And success is what I'm looking to achieve.

For more information on my work go to:
www.godvolcano.com
www.facebook.com/God.Volcano

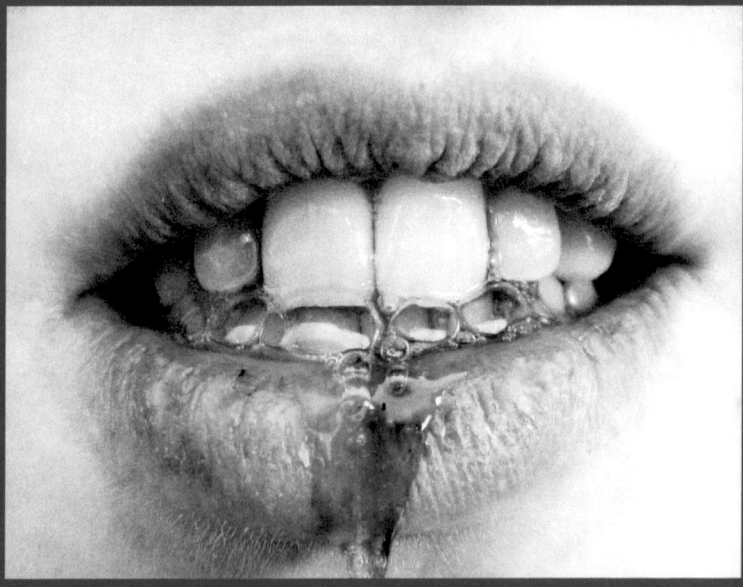

People You Must Meet, Places You Shouldn't Miss, Shows That Will Blow Your Minds: ALL OF WHICH ARE IN EUGENE, OREGON

By Tina Martinson

Eugene has one of the most diverse groups of talented artists, no bullshit Larry. Eugene is home to local artist, Sabrina Ridge, owner of The WAVE Gallery and Poppy & Moe clothing. Matt Dye, is the owner of Blunt Graffix who is hosting his own show in February of 2012.

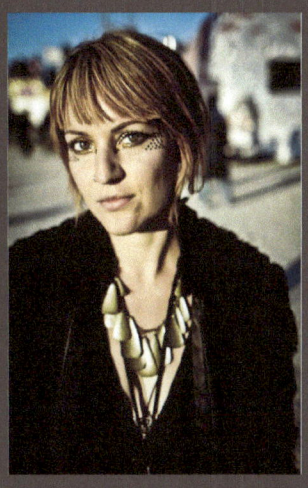

Sabrina Ridge is young, beautiful, fierce and very intelligent. Both of her parents are artists and Sabrina's talents were recognized at the ripe old age of five. Sabrina's kindergarten teacher immediately recognized her talents and told her parents that she must be encouraged. Sabrina continued to create during her middle school years primarily in pen and ink and her forte was bald, nude women. At one point her artistic taste would prove to be a bone of contention but this was not to daunt a young Sabrina and she continued to move forward with her art.

Sabrina is a bit of wanderlust, moving eleven times in seven years. Part of her travels took her to Wisconsin where she literally lived in the woods for a year without creating art. When I asked her about this she stated that she did not miss the creating process but that it was a very cathartic experience which helped her to move her art forward with her return to Eugene in 2006. Sabrina is a burner who has attended burning man and found it to be a very liberating experience.

In 2008, Sabrina was working at Gervais Coffee in Eugene, where she met Kelsie McGee, a co-worker who saw some of Sabrina's drawings. This was the beginning of Poppy & Moe, whose name is derived from Sabrina's poppy tattoo sleeve and Kelsie's maiden name which is Moe. They started buying equipment in 2009 and began selling t-shirts in 2010. McGee is a very talented woman who has a background in apparel, designing children's wear for Nordstrom. Together they make beautiful clothing that is in high demand in Eugene, Seattle, California and Japan. The line is nature and vintage inspired apparel for women. The use of sustainable products and garments is of the utmost importance. All artwork is original and printed by hand.

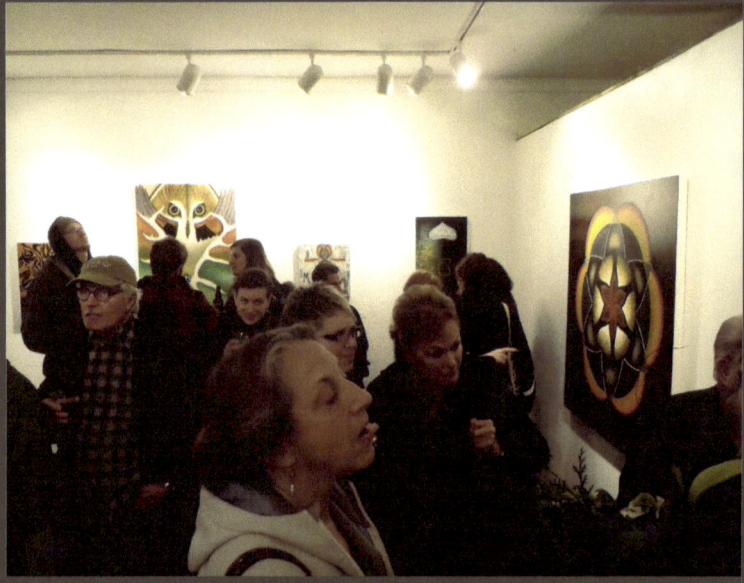

Sabrina started The WAVE artist collective to fill a need. Initially she wanted to start a monthly arts magazine for Eugene called The WAVE. When she realized how expensive it would be to run a magazine she decided against it but still felt like there needed to be some kind of glue in the arts scene in Eugene to keep people inspired and connected. "We all want to be more involved but there hadn't been a way to really stay connected" she said. The WAVE artist collective was an idea she had adopted after experiencing how efficiently people communicated on Facebook for Burning Man.

Sabrina wanted to, "...create a place to trade info, tools and knowledge and to create a place for them to communicate...[anything]...art related". Sabrina was a huge fan of Mo Bowen and her gallery, the Voyeur, in Eugene. Sabrina purchased the Voyeur from Mo in October 1, 2011 and The WAVE Gallery was born.

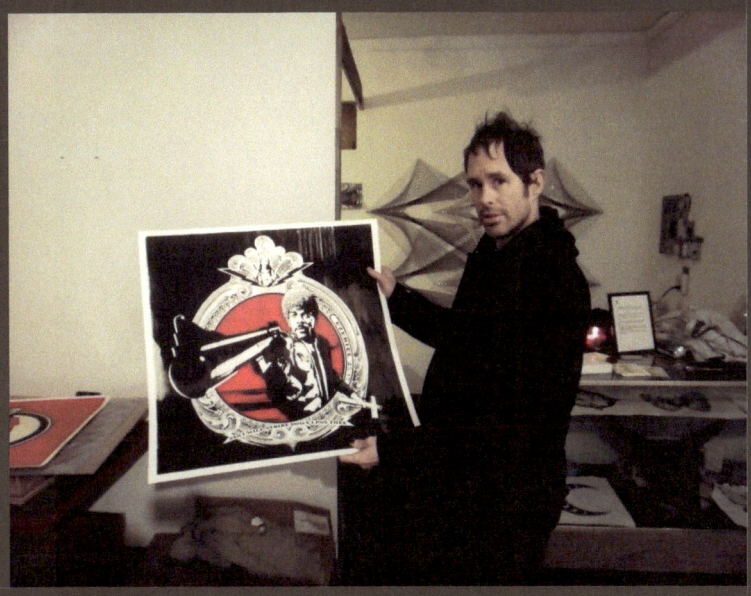

Now, let me tell you about Blunt Graffix.

Matt Dye is the owner of Blunt Graffix, and he is a very intense and intellectual person. Fear is his enemy and he devours it! I liken his persona to that of a neon sign for a dirty strip club, only brighter! Matt and Molly Mae own and run Blunt Graffix, as a working team. They both contribute to the design and silk-screening process as well as setting up shows like their upcoming *Dead Rock Stars*. They are both very proud parents of a very precocious one year old who already creates his own art!

Matt did not feel the burn of art growing up but while serving in the US Navy as an air traffic controller he discovered that he had a certain affinity towards the military's copy machines. It was also at this time that he was given several bootleg computer graphics programs and he began to monkey around with them. He discovered that they would keep reducing the size and quality of his images much to his consternation that he quickly outgrew them.

In 2000 he was creating logos for a surf shop in Hawaii but wasn't overly fond of the atmosphere. It was about a year later through a natural progression that he started Blunt Graffix. When I asked Matt which of the posters or bands were most notable to him he simply stated "none". But someone was defiantly taking notice and in 2004 he was in <u>The Art of Modern Rock</u>, a brash and colorful book that has become a must have for music and art lovers alike!

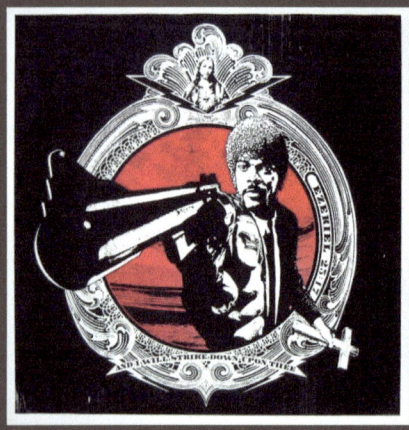

Matt continued to vigorously grow and expand Blunt Graffix. His work has been shown in New York, San Francisco, LA, Portland, Tokyo and Osaka. Matt has also participated in many group shows including Spoke Art in San Francisco and Mudob Gallery in Japan where his work consistently sells out. His piece *Ezekiel 25:17* is one of his hottest pieces and one of my personal favorites and yes, I own a small silk-screen print! It was created for a show called *Quintin vs.Coen III* and was part of a traveling art exhibition which ended in LA at the Beyond Eden Art Fair last October. It was Matt and Molly's constant participation in the group shows that gave them the confidence to give Blunt Graffix their own show!

Currently Blunt Graffix is gearing up for a one hell of a show, no bullshit Larry! The show it titled *Dead Rock Stars: A Tribute to the Mortal Gods of Sound* and it involves many diverse artists from all across the country and world. Artists such as Sean D'Anconia, Retro Outlaw Studios, Molly Mae Culligan ,Sabrina Ridge and of course Matt Dye. *Dead Rock Stars* had limited guidelines and the work was not juried. Matt and Molly chose the artist themselves and the only stipulation was that the work be their own creations; hand made by the artists' themselves. No digital prints.

Matt likes his prints to have a definite street art feel to them and will in fact make rough prints. I asked Matt how he came up with the idea of *Dead Rock Stars* and he stated that he likes to look for a connection. A twist in art that will make people uncomfortable .Then with a very sheepish grin he added, "Or what ever is getting on my nerves at the moment". It was at this time that I knew I was in the presence of greatness and a very naughty boy, and I was pleased.

Blunt Graffix do their best to be eco-friendly using only soy based solvents and water based ink. They also like to use what Matt calls "oops paints" House paints that have been rejected by whoever. Blunt Graffix is also looking to the future and plan on having many more shows and total world domination!

So pay attention kids! I'm telling you that Poppy & Moe, The WAVE Gallery and Blunt Graffix are where it's at....Get in on the ground floor and say "I was there!"

The opening reception for *Dead Rock Stars* will be February 2nd, 2012 in Eugene, Oregon at Blunt Graffix, a 2000 square foot artist studio that is located at 1040 Tyinn St #3, Eugene. Doors open at 6pm. The show runs through February 24th. The art will then move to THE WAVE Gallery, located at 547 Blair Blvd, Eugene, OR and will remain until late March.

You can find more info about Poppy & Moe at:
www.poppyandmoe.com
www.facebook.com/poppyandmoe

You can find more info about The WAVE Gallery at:
www.facebook.com/TheWAVEGallery

You can find more info about Blunt Graffix at:
www. bluntgraffix.com & www.modob.com

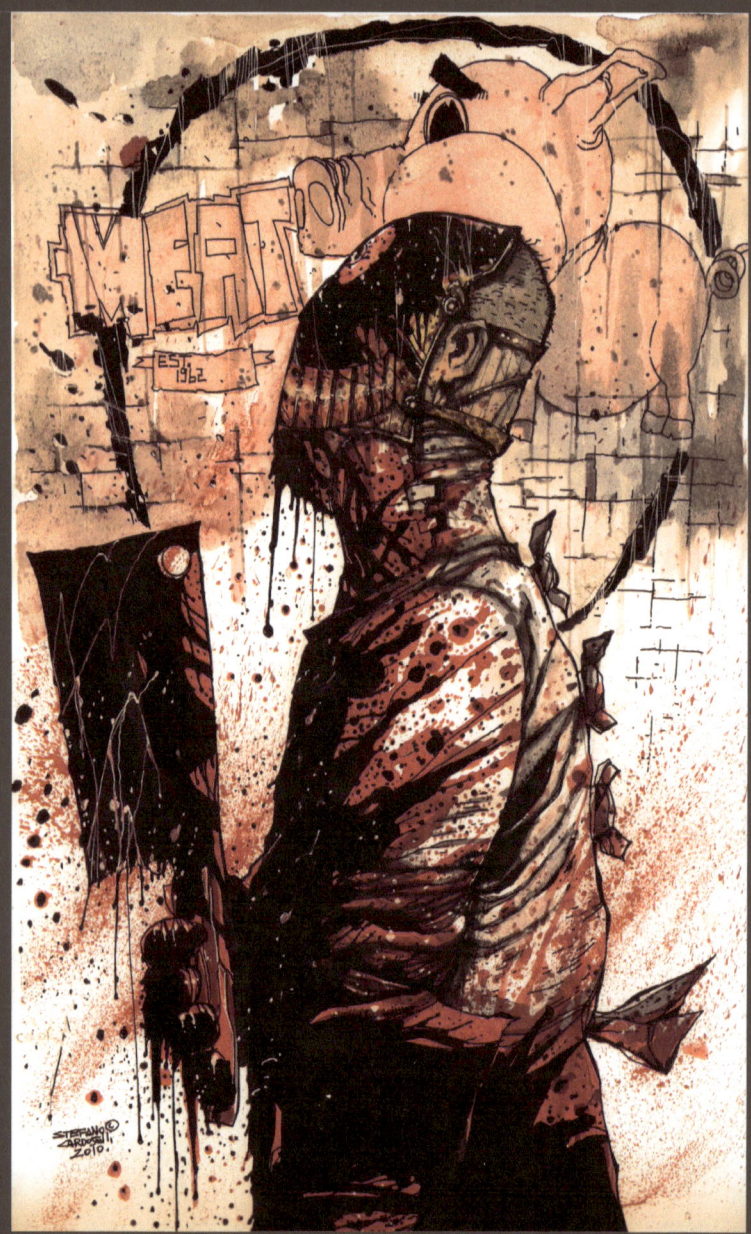

STEFANO CARDOSELLI: EXPORTED TO AMERICA

By EA Zine Staff

Our staff recently caught up with Italian illustrator Stefano Cardoselli and had a chance to ask him some questions.

EAZ: Tell us how you decided be become an illustrator; was it a life long passion or was it a skill you discovered in school?

SC: I started drawing when I was little, and I read a lot, too. Always loved drawing and become a comic artist,
I designed and wrote my first comic books when I was 10 to 11 years old... had some success among my relatives.
I've always drawn comics and have been drawing all time, but did not know at all how to send something to editors.

EAZ: Where did you attend art school and what was your focus of study?

SC: Art school here called, *Liceo Artistico* In Grosseto - Tuscany (near where I was born) and Comics-School in Rome

EAZ: What role did art school play in your career as a comic book illustrator?

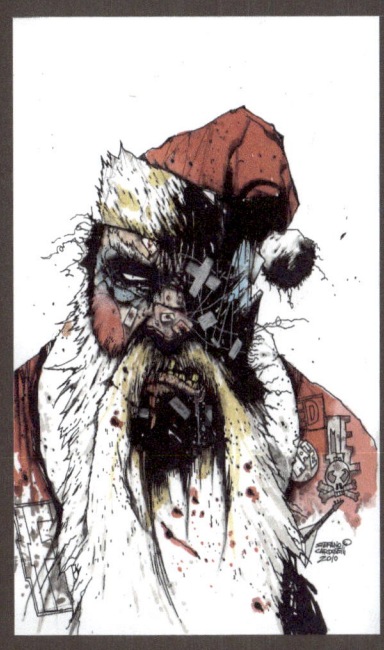

SC: Certainly *Liceo Artistico* was really important, I can not say the same for the school of comics, it was completely useless and without sense to me. I believe that a school of comics should prepare artists to work by providing tools, such as how we relate with how to send a submission or how to contact a publishers etc... this is not what happened. So I learned everything in the course of a direct experience.

EAZ: Tell us about your company and how you came to start it with your wife.

SC: Azurek Studios, is a comic-studio and the idea of it was born in 1998, created by me and my wife Rita, the official date of the birth date of 2001. It is the date of our first story in Heavy Metal magazine. We are a group of artists and we can provide complete book, story through artwork (pencils, inks, colors: hand made or digital and lettering).

We can also realize toys, t-shirts, and more recently also pins.

Rita is editor in chief and is responsible for the management and approval of projects and proposals, drawing and coloring as well as writing. I am co-editor and I see the submissions we receive from artists and colorists.

In fact, in the staff we have different colorists with different color styles, an English supervisor, a letterer, and an animator. The great thing is that we have collaborators from all around the world. I think Azurek has grown a lot, if you think about it, the studio was born on the benches of the school when there were only 2 employees, now we are 12...

EAZ: Have you shown any of your works in a gallery before?

SC: Here in Italy? Italy is a dead country, where art is considered a hobby, the comic is not considered at all, the funny thing is my first exhibition was made in the USA at Burger and Friends in Texas last summer, it was a great thing .

EAZ: What advice would you give to emerging illustrators?

SC: Always be yourself, humble and proud of your work.

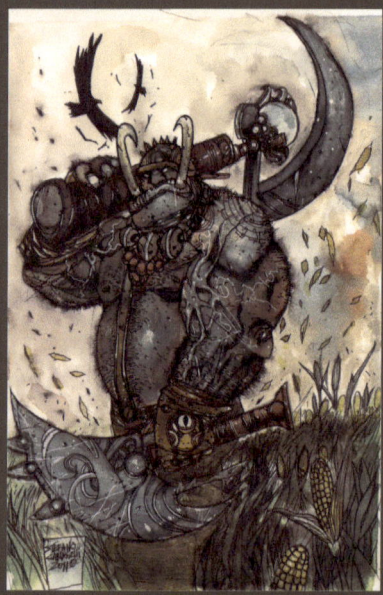

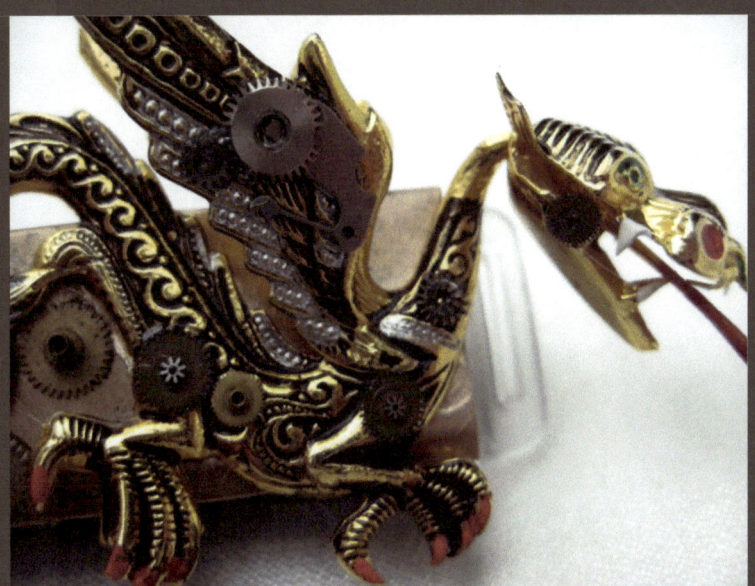

The New Face of Steampunk

By Autumn Anglin

I was raised in a very creative and inspiring household. My dad is a musician and worked for himself and my mom home schooled my brother and I while also working for herself. We were involved in the arts growing up which helped me decide to become an artist myself. I have always had a talent and drive to create things and I am a quick learner. Those talents have driven me to teach myself almost every skill I have. After being accepted into the program at the Fashion Institute of Technology in New York, I decided the fashion industry was too cut throat for me as I could not handle criticism and took it too personally.

I decided instead to pursue a Business Administration degree with a double minor in Economics and Marketing. I got my Bachelors degree in three years and moved on to a Masters in Applied Economics and a Masters in Economic History of Energy, neither of which were completed because my husband, Andrew and I moved and started a family.

In 2003, while I was working on my Masters degree in Jacksonville, Florida I started my first photography business. This was my first true art form that still has a special place in my heart. My Mom was always into photography and took great photos of my brother and I when we were kids. I borrowed her 35mm cameras when I was 13 and started taking pictures. During those years I traveled to a few different countries to take photographs and as a result they were show in several galleries in Florida. To pay for the art I photographed weddings. I loved doing weddings but they were always such hard work.

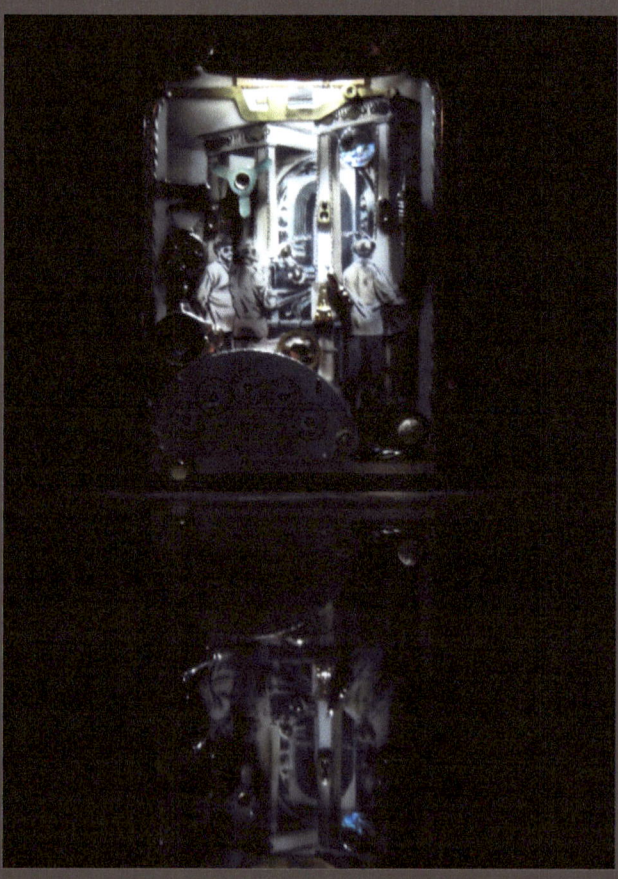

I love photography, but I am not one of those rigid photographers that think film is the only way. I am enamored with the digital era and the filters and graphic capabilities that come along with photo editing now.

At twelve years old, I was making jewelry and by the age of fourteen, I started designing and making all of my formal wear for weddings, Christmas events, prom and other special events. It always amazed my Grandmothers and Mom that I could just cut the fabric with out a pattern and it would turn out beautifully. By the time I turned 18, I was helping my local community theater make costumes for their plays. And I rarely sewed with a pattern, I would just cut the fabric to what I saw in my head.

These days if something interests me I get a bunch of books on it or watch as many YouTube videos as I can then I buy all the tools and get to work. I have tried my hand at everything from weaving to welding and am good at all of it. What amazes me is how most skills are interchangeable and it really takes an eye for design to ensure everything come together. All of these skills have grown and developed over the years to culminate into what I'm doing today.

[Steampunk Explained]

Steampunk is the genre my art has always had a place in, I just had not realized it. My mediums have always been old scrap or what most people would think of as trash. When my friend, Mac McGowan, introduced me to Steampunk as a Neo-Victorian industrial futurism, I was intrigued. I met Mac at the first Emerge I showed in and was instantly drawn to the man in the top hat that looked so theatrical and interesting. We got to know each other over the next few months and he encouraged me to embrace the designs of steampunk. For me Steampunk is an alternate history to the Victorian era that we can recreate now. What if the ornate Victorian age had the Technology of today or even the future? We would have people wearing corsets and top hats while riding on airships to the steam powered floating city all while checking their beautifully encased version of a smart phone. It is a fantasy but such a beautiful and versatile one. I believe Steampunk is still being developed and I am helping define it with my art.

[Find out more at: www.kimtag.com/autumnsteam]

[STEAMPUNK BY DESIGN]

The design inspiration for my gadgets and books is my huge stash of supplies. I never go into a project with a plan and can only create when I am surrounded by my little metal bits and pieces, books from the early 1900's and by leather working supplies. My stash looks like a pile of junk that should be tossed in the garbage but I see so much potential in those things. Spending days and weeks finding the perfect piece to accent a journal or gadget, I generally use what I have and when its gone I can't get another one. That is what makes my pieces so unique and hard to duplicate.

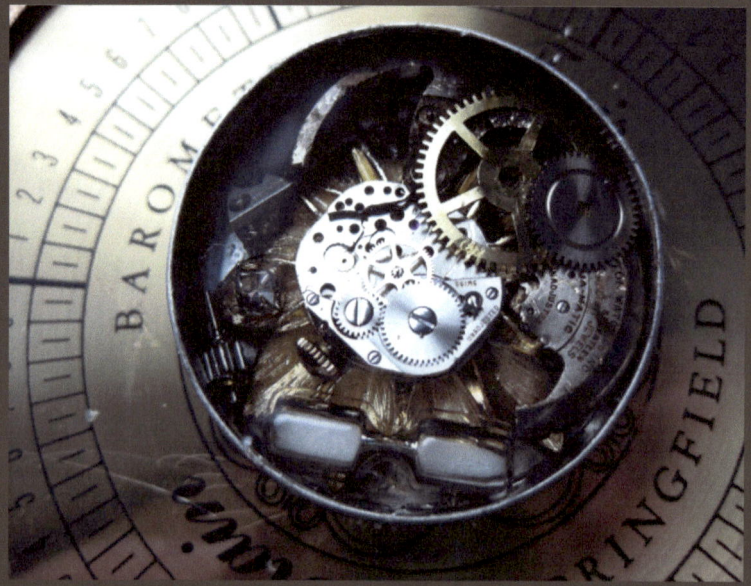

After discovering the Steampunk genre I knew it was a perfect fit for my vision as a fashion designer. I have always wanted to create fantastical, industrial, beautiful pieces of wearable art and now have the peramaters to do that. I started creating Steampunk clothing for our family because we needed something to wear to the Steampunk conventions. We got so many compliments I decided to make a line. Most of 2011 was focused on my Steampunk Fashions.

I managed to do 5 fashion shows this year. Wild Wild West Con in Arizona, Silverton Ladies Night Out at the Oregon

Gardens, RAW Natural Born Artists in Portland, Flux Magazine premier at the University of Oregon and Gear Con in Portland. They were all put together in a massive team effort by my talented models, a DJ friend who mixed the catwalk music and some very talented hair and makeup artists. Most of the audiences loved the show although as Avant-garde goes some people did not really understand it. My favorite show was the Flux Magazine premier although I loved working with the models at RAW.

I have shown my work in three gallery settings; at Emerge Oregon Art Series, the Timeless Talismen Gallery in Salem and the gallery at Steamcon III in Seattle.

I have found it easier to market my art by relying on social networking like Twitter, Facebook, Google+, Etsy, Blogger, and Kimtag. I have managed to work the system into making it so Autumn Steam is the first thing that pops up on a search on Google as well. I stopped participating in the Salem Saturday Market over a year ago. I now only participate in Emerge Underground, gallery shows and Steampunk events. I am really trying to push my online presence so I don't have to travel as much. Between booth fees for the event and staying out of town it is becoming more expensive to do a show. We rarely make our money back at any show. Our online presence is moving much faster for us.

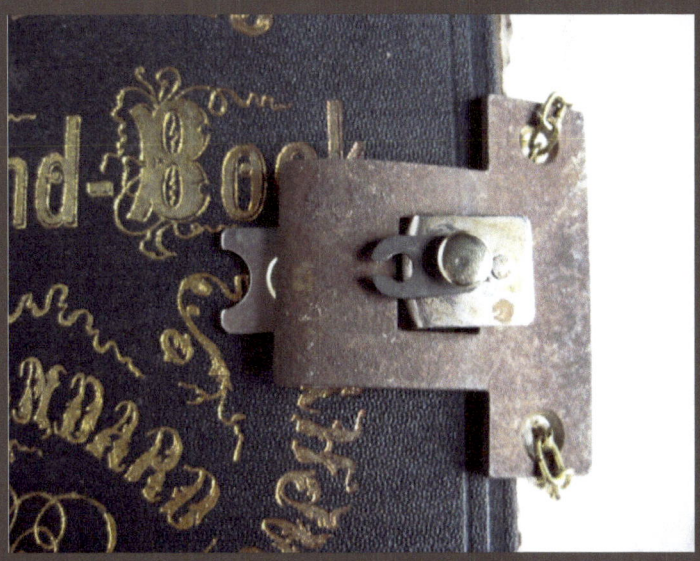

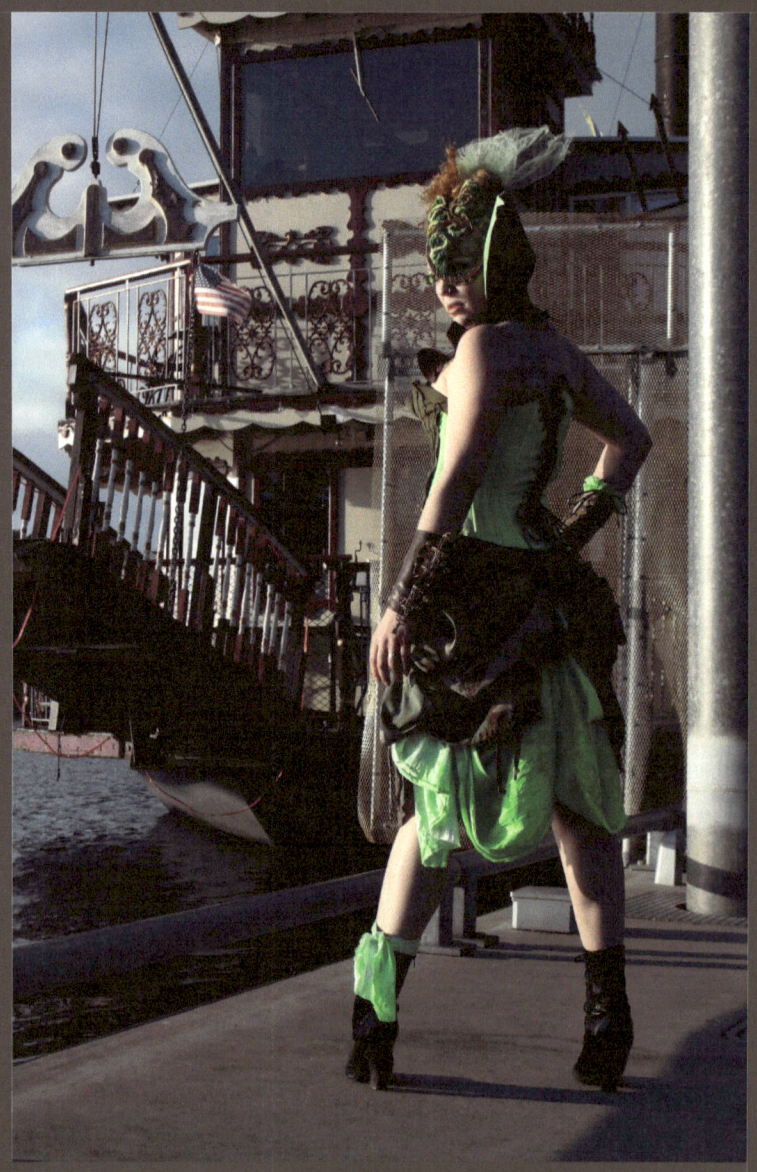

In the next five years my designs will evolve and grow as my interest do. I am hoping to have more time when my kids go off to school to really concentrate on my work. I have to say I am never short on ideas, just time. I would love to be recognized worldwide for my art and hopefully will have traveled to Asia to bring my fashion and vision there. My husband/collaborator and I are coming up with a plan now to get us on that side of the world!

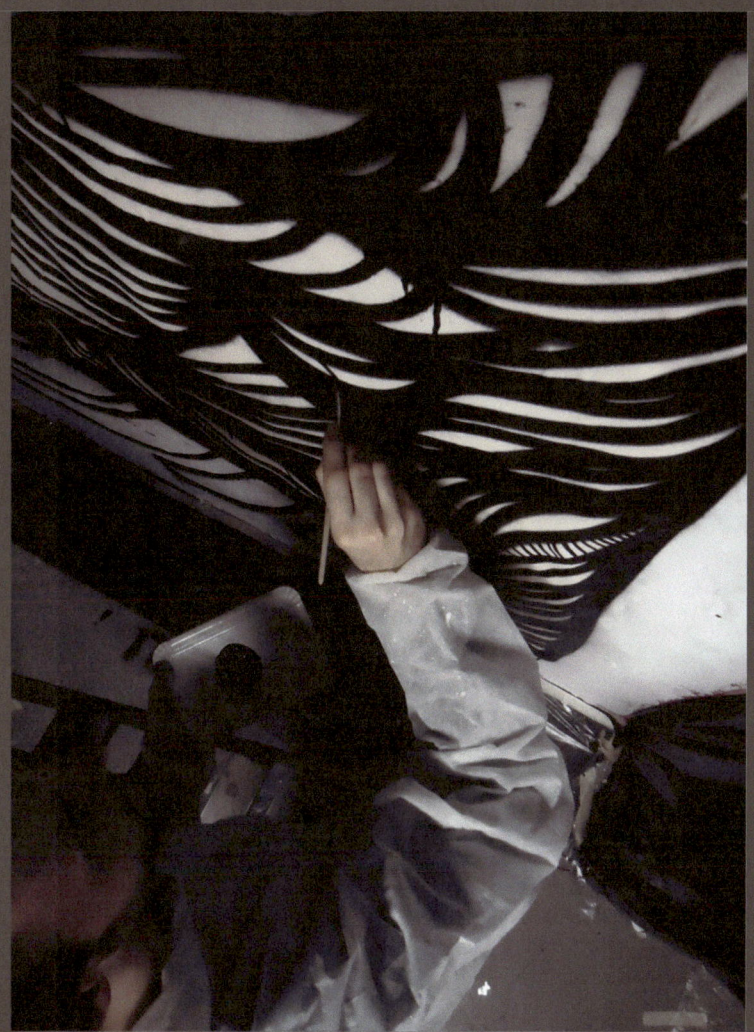

KEF: German Graffiti Artist

by Jonathan Boys

Born in Aachen, Germany, KEF has embraced his destiny as an up and coming street artist.

Street Art is a loose term thrown around these days by people both in the art world and outside of it. Many street artists are sticker artists these days and it is harder to find a sticker artist who knows his way around a can of Montana Gold. KEF is such an artist. He got his start early on painting "traditional graffiti" and that opened up doors for him to develop his characters that he paints now. He depends on the eyes of the creatures to draw in and mesmerize each viewer. His paintings are highly textural and are mixed with the feel of a woodblock print.

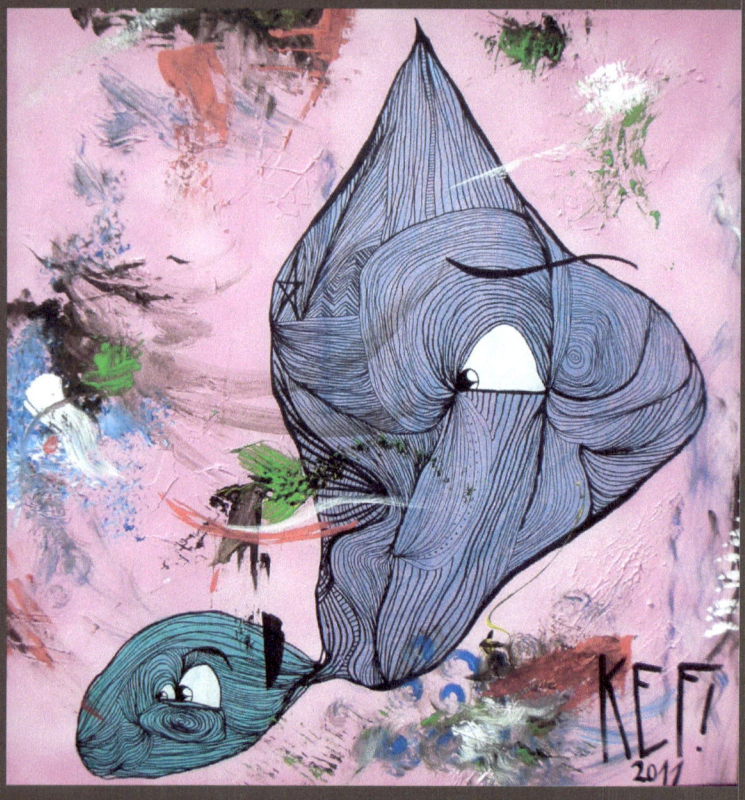

"I am using a mixture of techniques far from what's considered as normal, and I am trying to not have my surroundings affect me".

In 2011, KEF's work was part of Weserburg Museum for Contemporary Art's sixth International Sticker Awards.

As is typical for the street art scene KEF is also a electronic music producer which allows him to further expand his character base.

For more information on KEF go to:

www.kefart.de

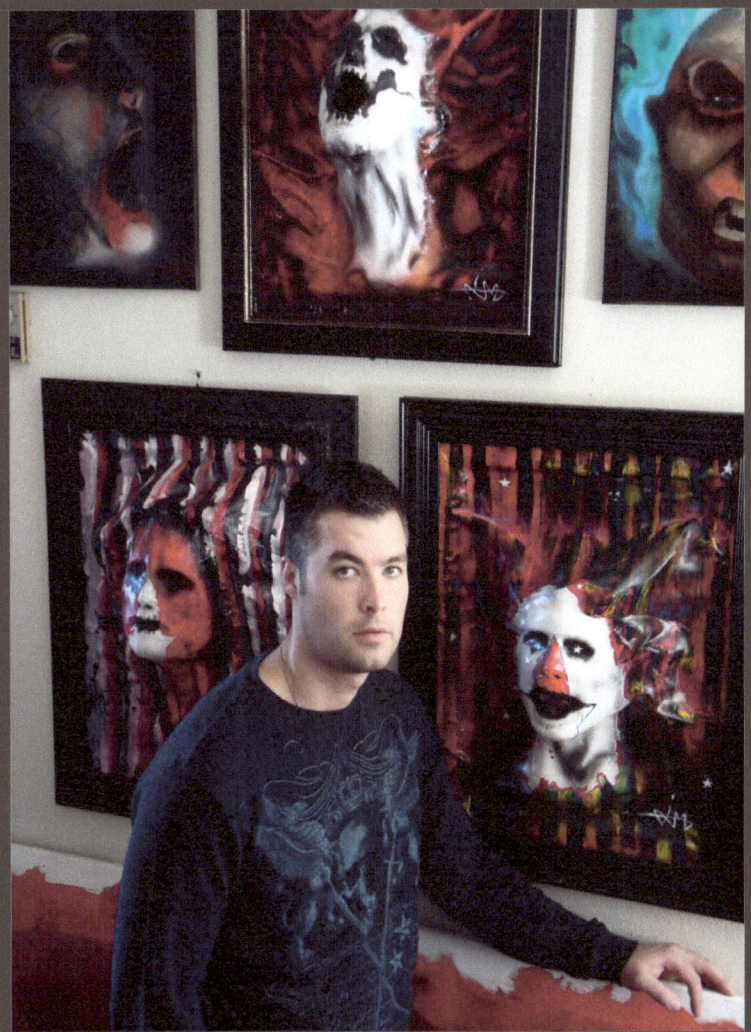

The Garage Mechanic of The Art World

By Jonathan Boys

I first met Aaron Molinsky at Emerge Oregon Art Series in Salem, Oregon, where he showed his life size mixed media fiberglass sculptures. His work is very unique, he is driven to make sure he is always creating groundbreaking art. Growing up in Canby, about half way in between Salem and Portland, he was brought up in a hardcore religious setting in which art and music were frowned upon. This is a major influence in his work today.

These days he lives just outside of San Francisco with his wife Kezia and their kiddo, on the campus of Menlo College. It was Kezia who got initially pushed him toward art, she bought him his first set of paints. He gives her full credit for starting his art career. "My work expresses sadness, anger, frustration and not feeling you have a voice...these are real valid feelings that deserve attention in art. Not just the happy rainbows. It purges these feelings from me and hopefully lets the viewer know we are together with those feelings. The end goal? Create beauty from sadness", explains Molinsky.

Because his studio size is significantly smaller since the move to California, he has switched his focus from sculpture back to painting. He is fine tuning his work by drawing on techniques he has seen in J Slattum's work. By doing this he can tie it back into his sculpture work, with an end goal of a large body of work of mixed media sculptures that will blow people's minds.

In August of 2011, Molinsky showed for the second time at The Gallery Zero in Portland. He unveiled his largest painting entitled *The Coward's Path*. It is about suicide, his take on someone's choice to take their life. "Just because life is shitty, you're just kinda opting out and then leaving everybody with your mess...the lady licking the skull, she was embracing death which signified her embracing death".

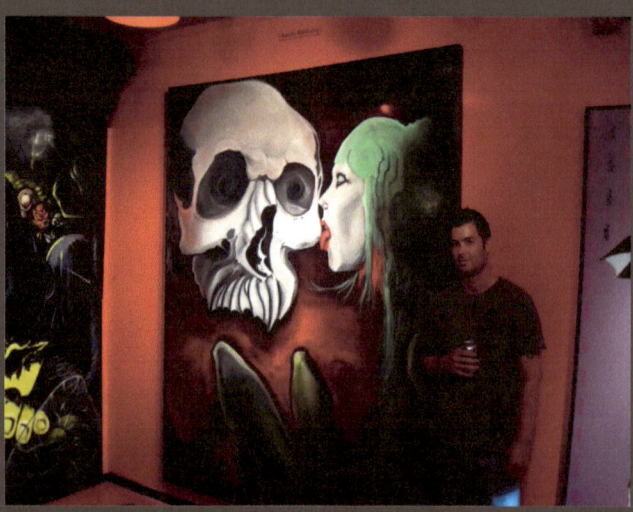

Recently, he entered a traditional plein-air contest at Menlo College and they awarded his work with the Best in Show title. He was really encouraged that he was able to go up against seasoned fine art painters and show his skills off. He referred to himself as "the garage artist of the art world" because he is completely self taught. Part of his award is a show featuring his work and the second and third place winners. So he is going to introduce his own style into this traditional art show.

He has been developing a brand new series of paintings that he will unveil for this show entitled *Skullscapes*. "I love painting skulls but everybody's doing them right now and nobody's really making anything that unique anymore, it's all kind of the same stuff. It's awesome, but it's kinda getting old. So, that kinda gave me an idea of going to a different level and showcasing a traditional landscape painting with a big fat bloody skull in the middle of it!"

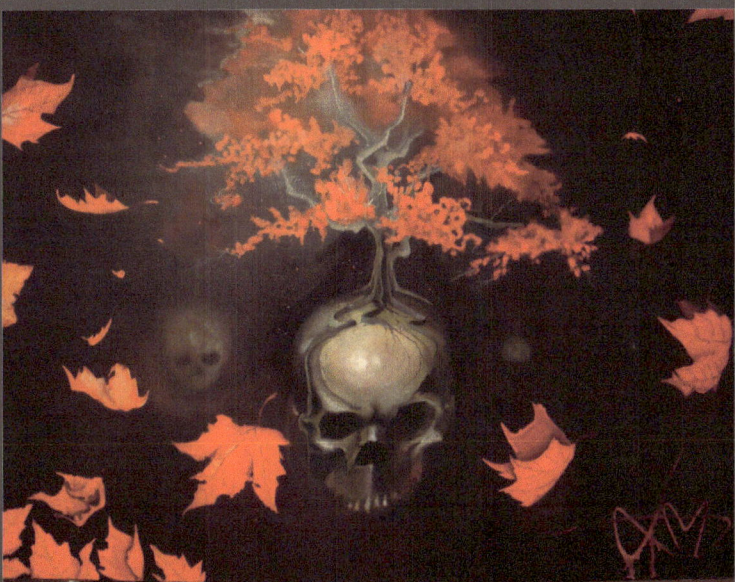

So how did he come upon this plein-air contest? His wife, who works for Menlo College saw it and urged him to enter. "I was thinking, well yeah that might be good, try something new and try a new crowd. The cool thing was that my stuff was really well received by everyone, I didn't get anybody that was like 'ugh that's terrible', everybody was like 'oh that's awesome'...I don't have anything but good stuff to say about the school because they allow people like me to enter that and they don't have any prejudice over what my normal style is. It's just about making a good painting and [them] showcasing for you. That's awesome that they'll actually do that when most places are gonna go 'who are you, and who did you train under or where did you go to school'."

He said when he was in Portland he felt like the doors were really beginning to open up and he was getting connected to people, but since his move he's had to start over. I asked him about his experience showing at The Gallery Zero. "I thought it was really good, just because of the fact that it's really hard to find a gallery that's willing to show my stuff and actually be excited even. Normally I don't get a response from a gallery normally, especially in the Willamette Valley when I lived there, it was kind of a thanks but no thanks. There I really thought that even if the clientele doesn't come in and buy the pieces at least there was people there appreciating it and I was getting exposure for sure."

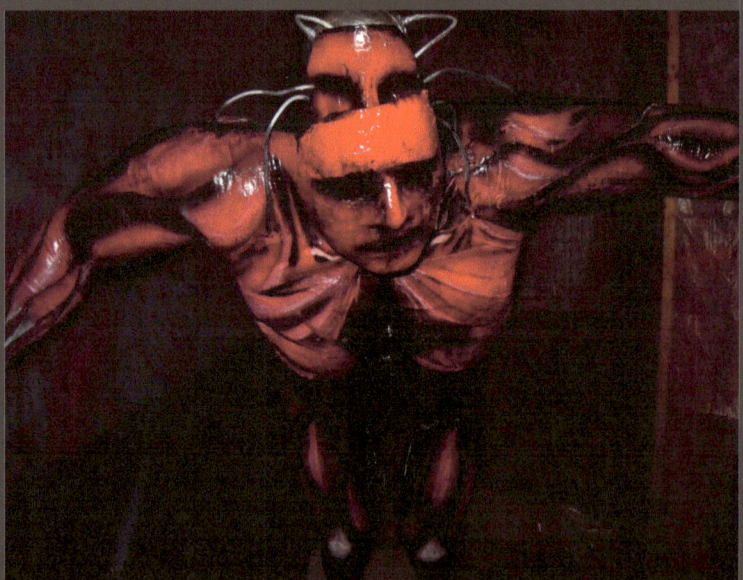

["The Lost," took Aaron one year to create and it is made up of 85 individual molds cast from his own body. It is counter weighted at the foot of the sculpture so that it stands upright.]

I had a conversation with Molinsky about the genre of dark art and the business of attracting attention to it. He told me, *"There are people that like the stuff, I mean there are so many artists that are making it there have got to be just as many people that enjoy that kind of art, the darker stuff, [who] can appreciate it. Just trying to get the word out there and trying to get exposure for it is the hugest thing."*

In my opinion many artists at the top of the genre in America should be shown in Germany, the Czech Republic, Russia, places that would really appreciate the work. The US is still so conservative, there are only a hand full of galleries willing to step out and show this kind of art. Aaron summed it up well:

"It is weird most people get into art for freedom of their thoughts and ideas and being able to express them to people, yet only if it's the OK ideas that are accepted within the guidelines. How many times can you paint the same thing? It's great looking, but there were guys doing the same thing 100 years ago, doing the same thing you are doing right now. There is nothing different about it, you haven't upped the ante or changed anything. You've just repeated what you've seen and then taught as art. You've not pushed any boundaries or tried to further your own capabilities, you've just been OK with making the same thing because that's what people are OK with. Because that matches their couch and it doesn't scare them and doesn't make them upset, because it doesn't question their ideals so that's what they like."

As Confucius said, "The scholar who cherishes the love of comfort is not fit to be deemed a scholar."

You cannot find Molinsky's work on Facebook. He's adamantly against it, for now. *"I kind of like to do my own thing, I guess that was too much of what everybody else was doing...it was kind of like a screw you to the mass marketing, but maybe I screwed myself I don't know. Twitter is short and sweet and that's kinda the way I like it!"*

www.twitter.com/AaronMolinsky

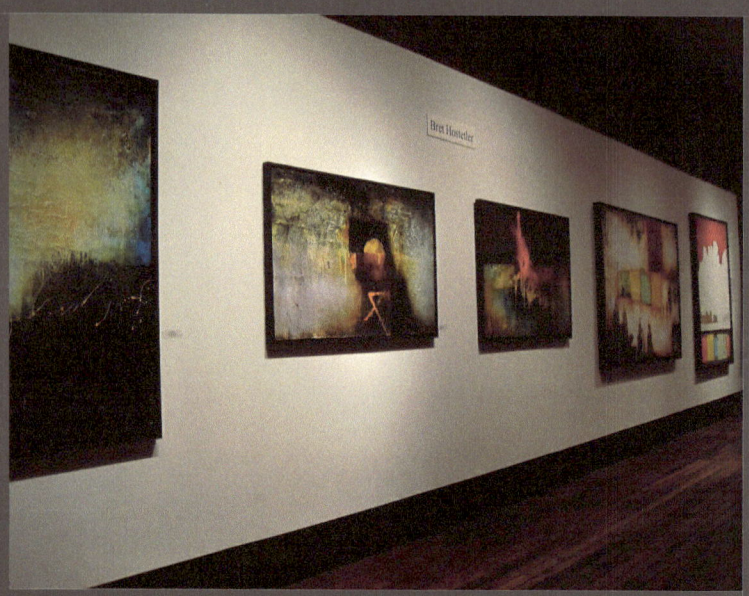

GRAETER ART GALLERY: The Bar Has Been Raised

By Jonathan Boys

August 9, 2011, was a normal day for the rest of us, S&P downgraded the US government's credit rating, we were trying to find hope in what seemed to be constant economic despair. For John Graeter, it was a great day, he had just signed a three year lease on his new gallery space. As I watched his Facebook pictoral updates on the construction process I began to get more and more excited.

So many galleries open and struggle to make it. What it all comes down to whether the owner knows not only how to curate a good show and have a cool opening reception, but whether they understand how to sell art.

John Graeter is the embodiment of the term, gallerist. Going into his new gallery space he had already developed a group of collectors and is actively developing new collectors, something missing in most galleries in the US these days. He not only has an eye for great art he has a following of great artists so he doesn't have to go far to find new works. It was a calculated move to put the gallery in old Chinatown, as it's still downtown but it is separated from the main body of galleries in the Pearl District.

I attended the Graeter Art Gallery's first opening and was stunned. The art spoke volumes. The space was packed, the DJ was mixing some chill house music, his wine bar buzzed with activity. I went through careful to view each piece and really take it in, a hard task in a crowded space. One artist's works really stuck out to me, Theodore Holdt.

Holdt's 72" x 72" piece, *Space Girl*, sucked me right in like a tractor beam. Whether intentional or not it had elements of Hieronymus Bosch's *The Garden of Earthly Delights*, painted roughly 510 years ago. The piece was intentional chaos, it was beautiful and haunting all together. As to be expected the work sold.

I returned once again, camera in hand to the January showing of *A Nashville to Portland Skyline Boulevard*. Bret Hostetler's work was brilliant. Each piece was uniquely different yet tied together by the underpinnings of his five personal guidelines to create art.

Refreshment was my favorite of his works in the show. It seemed to have been painstakingly covered in layer after layer of paper and paint. His mixture of blues and earth tones are reminiscent of Rembrandt's work, it doesn't appear to be intentional but it is remarkable. If the viewer were to look back at *The Mill* and *The Bridge* it would be an uncanny comparison to colors. Hostetler rounds out the work with dabbles and throws of yellow, which is part of what draws the viewer in to the piece. His style is that of a seasoned painter, all the while he is just in the beginning stages of his career.

Standing in the back of the gallery I admired a large piece of bricolage, *Untitled 12* by Andrew Enna. It was made up of pieces of tin from old signs. To create his pieces he collects things and then surrounded by these items he allows them to speak to him, to come together and create each work.

The Graeter Art Gallery has helped to restore hope to Portland's art scene in my opinion. Graeter has set the bar for this next generation of gallerists, proving that you can still have a world class gallery that not only shows the work of exciting emerging artists, but one that sells it.

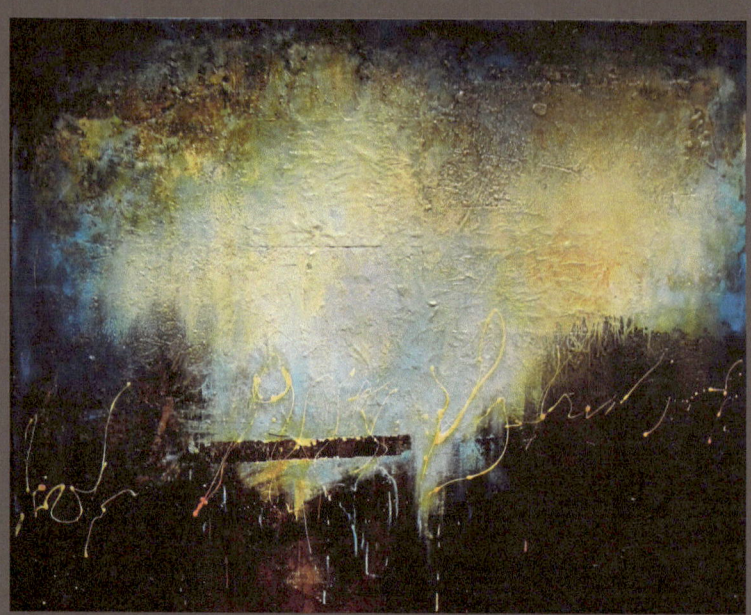

Refreshment by Bret Hostetler 2011

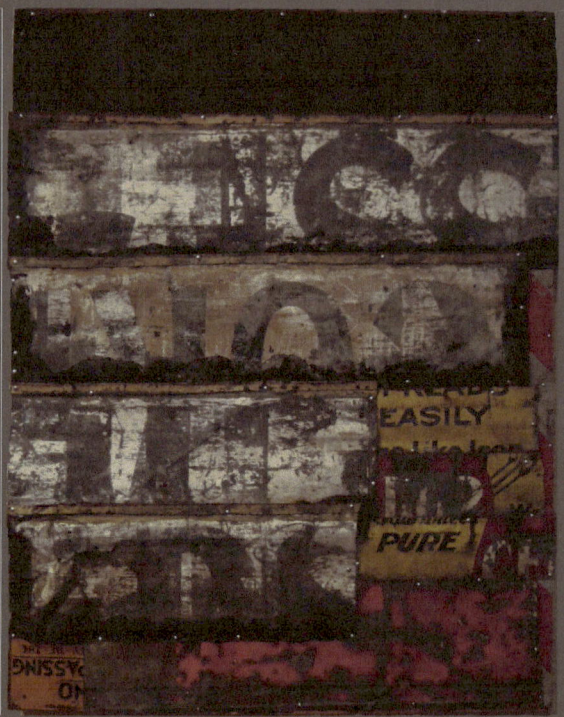

Untitled 12 by Andrew Enna

For more information on the Graeter Art Gallery go to:
www.graeterartgallery.com

DEVELOPING THE NEXT GENERATION OF COLLECTORS

By Jonathan Boys

For the past 30 years the art business has been on cruise control. I honestly believe that gallery owners and art dealers thought the Baby Boomers were the end game for the business and never bothered to strategize for the future.

Now let me clarify that there are different levels of art collectors out there. And there are three tiers the the gallery business: high, middle and low. Typically the high and middle market galleries are "Blue Chip". Blue chip galleries sell art to collectors who are more often than not investing in art from more of a financial standpoint and less of a "wow that's going to look great in my dining room" perspective.

When we hear about the art business boom it's not the low to middle markets making the headlines. That news is strictly for the high market selling in auction houses and international art fairs. That part of the art business is golden. It's the non blue chip mid to low market I am making reference to.

If you were to take a snapshot of the mid market in 2012 as opposed to the one in 2005 you would see a remarkable difference. Many mid market blue chip galleries were forced to close after the economic crisis started in late 2008. There are countless reasons for this but one of the biggest things in 2009 was that the industry was reporting that the average sale price for art was $1,000. Wait, what? How could that have ever happened? It happened because the economic woes of the marketplace scared the Baby Boomers, which resulted in them tightening their belts and truth be told many of them were having to return to work because they could not afford retirement.

And so the decline in the mid market began. No one really knows how the low market galleries were effected by the downturn, there isn't much data available, just personal interactions with gallery owners and curators.

I'm confident that most people do not realize that in an average US city the majority of art galleries fit into the low marketplace. Now if you were to go to a large city like LA, NYC, or Chicago, you'll find the majority of galleries are mid to high market blue chip. In a large city, real estate rates are higher and a low market gallery cannot remain viable, pay overhead, etc, without a set source of income.

It would be helpful to describe a typical low market gallery. It is a space generally that shows local and regional artists, depending on the part of the nation it is located they plan their shows six months to a year out or they plan month to month, they depend on purchases from the general public and generally have a handful of collectors. Their pricing structure demands they sell individual works for under $5,000. They are owned by artists, collectors and art activists. Most only sell a few pieces a month, the gallery owners work a second job or they have a partner that funds the space to keep it in operation. In short if the gallery was to stay open based on art sales, it would have to close. Low market galleries are very popular because they give local artists a chance to have their work shown in public.

So what's wrong with having a low market gallery that only sells from time to time? Aren't they contributing to the health and culture of society? The simple answer is yes they are a viable part of our society strictly from a cultural perspective. But when it comes down to simple economics they are doing a disservice to the community. Artists begin to lose hope that they will ever sell work and have anything more than a part time career in art. The community in turn falsely is lead to believe, by these galleries, that work is being sold. But then there is another negative that follows suit, no sales typically means a low market gallery closes its doors, so the community then begins question whether the visual arts are viable in their town. All of this is simply avoidable.

If a gallery wants to show art without selling it then it would be my recommendation to start a non profit contemporary art museum. Otherwise, make a plan to develop a new group of collectors.

What is a collector?

Simply stated they are a person who buys a work of art because they see value in the piece and the artist. A blue chip collector not only sees the value of the work, they see the potential for the work to be sold for a higher price at a later date. The blue chip collector is purchasing nationally recognized artists for the most part although there are exceptions to the rule.

So what needs to happen for low market galleries to begin selling to new collectors? Education.

The general public is the potential collector base for a low tiered gallery. You might say, "The average Joe isn't going to buy art and more than likely they can't afford it". You would be wrong if you did say it. Americans spend their paychecks on luxury items every day. What do we need to live? Food, clothes, transportation and a place to sleep. Everything else is extra. People don't bat an eye about going to see a first run movie on a date or with the family and spending $20 to $100. They also go to the bar, they smoke cigars and cigarettes, they play the lottery.

And what is the common thread for all of those things? They are temporary luxuries that don't last.

What if we were to educate the public that they could own art that will last potentially for generations if it is well maintained, would they spend less on temporary luxury goods? What if in that education, people learned that they could effect a change in the local economy by purchasing art from a local artist instead of factory produced "art" from a big box retailer?

How you begin the process is up to you. I would recommend that you partner with other galleries in your town and work together through the process. Sure you may have to partner with people you don't see eye to eye with, but remain focused on the end goal, consistent sales. If you look at markets in the US that have embraced this ideology you find a united front for the arts, a strong community of successful career artists, and a strong sense of community pride.

This is just the starting place of something revolutionary in the low marketplace in America. Now that you realize you are holding the ball, it's time to get to work.

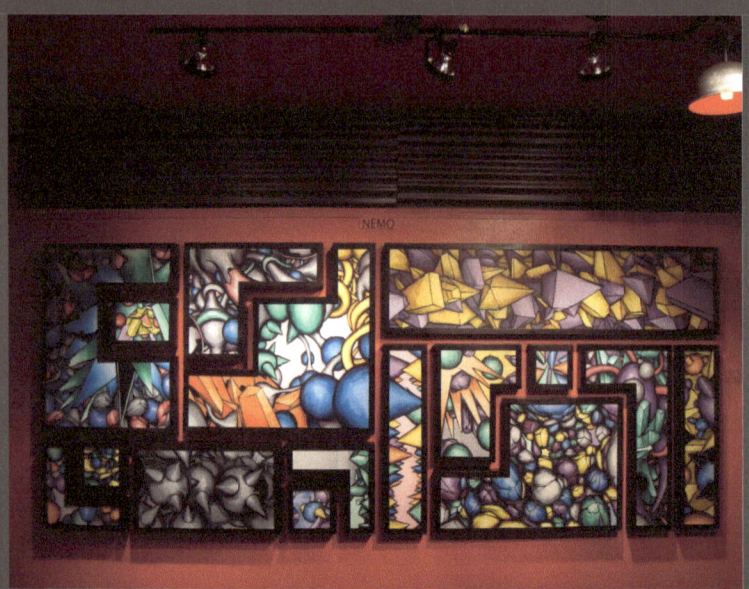

THE GALLERY ZERO: Small Gallery, Huge Art!

By Jonathan Boys

The first time I went to an opening at The Gallery Zero was April 1, 2011. My friend's Deklun and Pace were playing there and they invited me and my wife. As soon as I stepped inside the wow factor was overwhelming. The entire space is red, red walls, red floors, red ceiling. And it make the art pop off the walls.

One thing that I detest about contemporary art galleries are the solid white walls. The white actually creates a negative atmosphere for displaying art. Don't believe me? Please get up right now and head to the closest art museum that shows art from the 19th century or earlier. When you get there tell me what color the walls are. That's right, they typically are not white. The concept of white walls comes from minimalism, it is as if the contemporary art world is taking display cues from the Shakers.

After walking though the gallery and seeing all the art, Pace Rubadeau took me to the back to meet one of the two owners. Randy stood their talking up the space to a group of people and Pace introduced me. To my surprise Randy shook my hand and with a big smile he told me, "Jonathan, it's nice to finally meet you I've been following your work on Facebook for some time now." Well that got my attention for sure.

My wife, Charity, and I liked one artist in particular. What is significant about that is my tastes in art are typically wild and hers are tame. Nemo's work was intriguing to us. All of his work is bright, bold colors filled with geometric shapes, it is very robotic looking. That coupled with the shaped canvases and thick black frames all hung to create one large piece. The genius is that a collector could buy it as one piece or in pieces.

I don't think I've seen a gallery before that is almost completely devoted to graphic artists. It is a unique art gallery. One that people in Portland generally don't know about. Randy and Jim have been in business for three years, but they have been three long years struggling to find a public voice in the sea of galleries that makes up Portland's art scene.

To say, I've been unimpressed with the mainstream art scene in Portland so far is an understatement. It's a city teaming with extraordinary artists with a group of "art conservative" galleries showing artists who have been creating the same tired art for thirty years. But there is a group of galleries that have been busy for the past few years trying to gain back some of the ground claimed by the above group and the Gallery Zero is among them.

Randy Young is no stranger to the art world. He managed a few galleries in Beverly Hills and LA. He has represented some of the great contemporary artists of the 20th century.

He and Jim Lowry go way back. Jim, a film maker by trade wrote and directed a movie called "Bad Trip" in 1988. Randy co-starred in it. If you are interested you can purchase and watch it on Amazon.com. After the movie was released Randy decided to stay in LA to try to continue his career as an actor. Over time he realized it wasn't in the cards so he transitioned into a career in the gallery business.

Flash forward to 2008, Randy found himself returning to Portland with the idea to transform Jim's computer repair shop into a gallery to showcase graphic artists. They teamed up with Todd and Mary Millar to renovate the space. It was Todd and Mary who came up with that bold red look. Todd even designed and built the Gallery Zero light boxes you see on both sides of the door as you enter the space.

If you attend any opening you will no doubt be met by Randy, who is to put it mildly, passionate about his gallery and his artists, you will hear a theme. He will remind you that, "No one does it like we do", "it's all about presentation", "each show is consistently better than the last", "the walls are filled with iconic imagery". The artists that show there are equally as passionate.

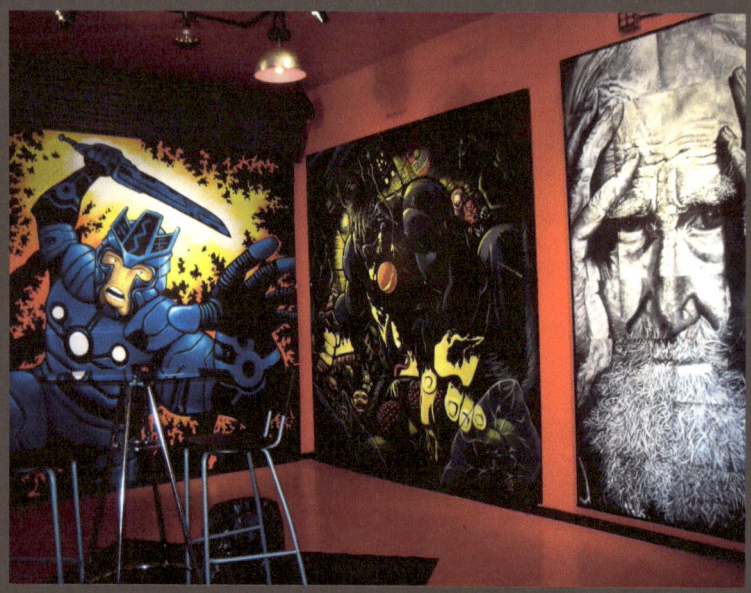

I intentionally attended the January 7th opening of the *Great Graphics Show* so I could grab some shots for this piece. I wasn't prepared for what they had hanging. I glanced at what seemed like a large installation of 2D art and walked through the gallery. Many of the pieces I had seen before, by Ben Perkins, Damien Zari and Joni Yates. But as I came around the corner I woke up. There in front of me was a massive installation of 91 paintings by Portland artist Jae Burlingame.

He told me that he used to sketch a lot when he was a kid but never took it seriously. "People tell you, paint what you know. I know movies, video games, cartoons...so I'm painting that". He has been painting for one and a half years and you would never know it. He started painting as a hobby to fill his time, he had been fired from a big box hardware store for a comment he made on his Facebook page. The first piece he did for this series was a Stormtrooper from Star Wars. He painted the background first and the color bled over into the white area on the canvas and after painting the outline he thought "man that looks good, that's how I'm going to do them all". He said that if he hadn't have painted the Stormtrooper which is white with black highlights, none of the other paintings would have happened. That was the first piece he sold.

One night while drunk with his friends he made the claim that he would paint 100 of them. Much to his friends' surprise he more than completed the task. It took him four and a half months to complete. Amazingly this was his third show. He was painting at a street fair in the rain and the owners of Salon 419 asked him if he would show his work in their salon. He showed his first 35 there and then he showed all 100 at Milepost 5. The curator of that show lives around the block from the Gallery Zero and talked to Randy about showing the pieces there.

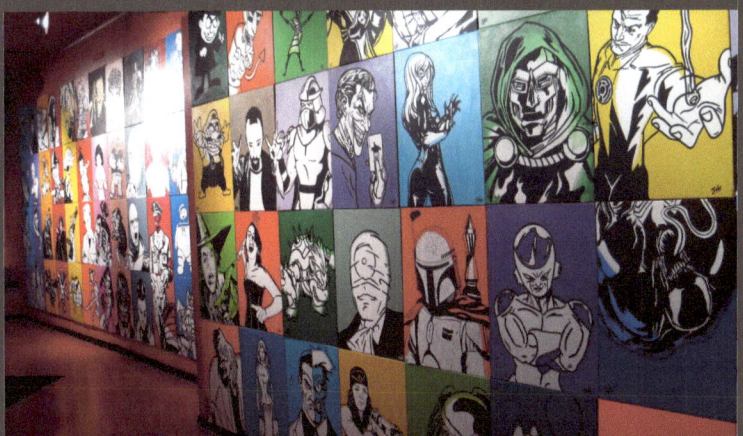

He sold 11 pieces the opening night at Milepost 5 at $200 each, which is not bad for his second time out.

"The reason I chose to do villains instead of heroes is they are so much more dynamic, more free willed and able to be crazy. And it's more compelling. If it wasn't for the villains, then your heroes wouldn't matter. So it's actually giving them the spotlight that they deserve. And every villain is a hero in their own story."

I asked him what he has in store for his next show. He's

working on a large scale tribute to his original Stormtrooper painting. "The idea behind it is, Stormtroopers are clones of each other. But from the moment of cloning they all have individual experiences, they're all, you know, everywhere. So they are all going to be different colors, hand painted, so they're going to be individually flawed and individually colored, but the second you step back from it they are all going to look the same. So they are going to lose their individuality just by taking a step back."

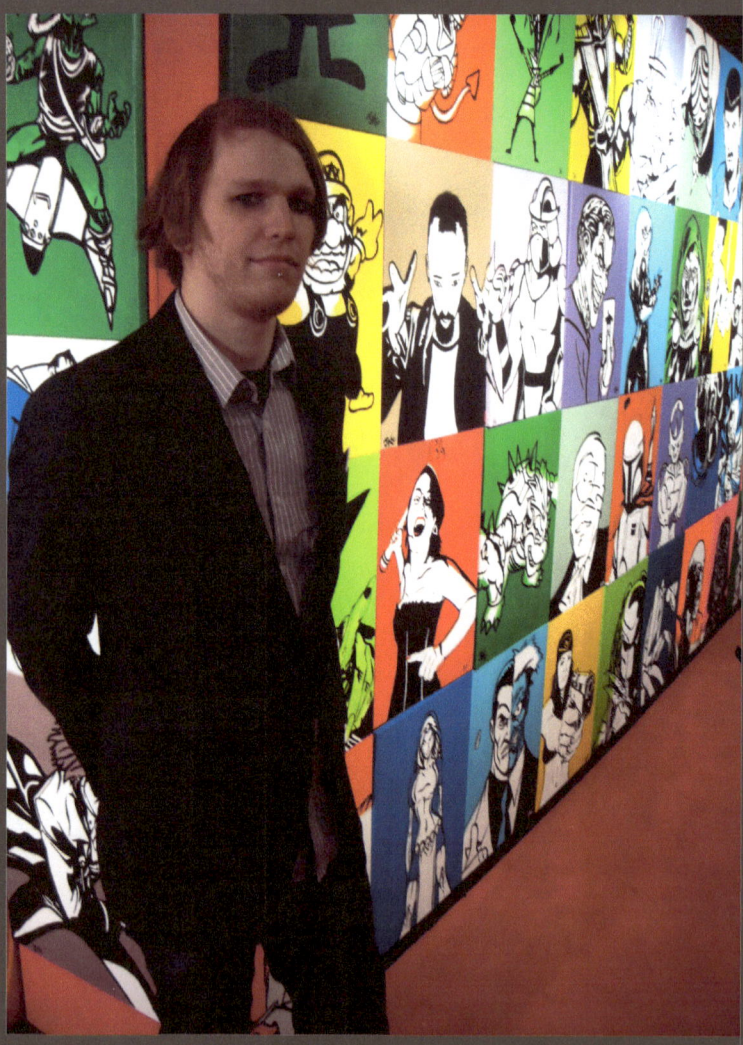

For more information on The Gallery Zero go to:
www.thegalleryzero.com

I would like to give special thanks to Emerging Artist Magazine's volunteer writers, editors, photographers and critics. You have taken ownership in this project. You are all helping to create something meaningful for this new generation of artists, collectors and art lovers. You mean the world to me.

I would also like to thank Rick Ahrens at Sticky Rick's. His passion to see artists be great and give them a vehicle to get their work around the world is awesome. Because of his partnership with EA Zine he helped give us a voice. If you need stickers please purchase them at www.stickyricks.net

PHOTO CREDITS:

In Review: Semantics Gallery's "distance between _____."
[approaches to contemporary drawing]
Photographs by Daniel Wolper

And The River Will Rise Up
Photographs by Samantha Hulbert

People You Must Meet, Places You Shouldn't Miss, Shows That Will Blow Your Minds: All Of Which Are In Eugene, Oregon
Photographs by Tina Martinson, Teddy Saunders & Blunt Graffix

Stefano Cardoselli: Exported to America
Illustrations by Stefano Cardoselli

The New Face of Steampunk
Photographs by Autumn Anglin

KEF: German Graffiti Artist
Photographs by KEF

The Garage Mechanic of The Art World
Photographs by Aaron Molinsky & Jonathan Boys

Graeter Art Gallery The Bar Has Been Raised
Photographs by Jonathan Boys

The Gallery Zero: Small Gallery, Huge Art!
Photographs by Jonathan Boys